This book is published strictly for historical purposes.
The Naval and Military Press Ltd
expressly bears no responsibility or liability of any type,
to any first, second or third party, for any harm,
injury or loss whatsoever.

SCIENTIFIC
UNARMED COMBAT

SIR ALAN ROSE, Q.C.
Chief Justice of Ceylon

SCIENTIFIC UNARMED COMBAT

The Art Of Dynamic Self-Defence
The Ancient Asian Pyscho-Physical Study

by

R. A. VAIRAMUTTU

Master of "Cheena-Adi" and "Ju-Jutsu" Self-Defence Arts
Founder and Chief Instructor,
School of Dynamic Self-defence

Foreword by

Hon. Sir Alan Edward Percival Rose, Kt., Q.C.,
M.A., LL.B., Barrister-at-Law, Chief Justice of Ceylon

Illustrated

The Naval & Military Press Ltd

Published by

The Naval & Military Press Ltd
Unit 5 Riverside, Brambleside
Bellbrook Industrial Estate
Uckfield, East Sussex
TN22 1QQ England

Tel: +44 (0)1825 749494

www.naval-military-press.com
www.nmarchive.com

In reprinting in facsimile from the original, any imperfections are inevitably reproduced and the quality may fall short of modern type and cartographic standards.

FOREWORD

It is with pleasure that I commend this book to the attention of the able-bodied citizens of this island. Not only are the contents instructive, but of definite value to anyone of us who may find himself confronted, unexpectedly enough, by some such situation as is so effectively dealt with by the author. The value of this type of exercise is that it is unnecessary for the practitioner to be a man or woman of unusual muscular development. Any person of reasonable physique whose reflexes are normally efficient should have little difficulty in mastering the defensive technique described in the book and excellently illustrated by the numerous photographs.

Practice, no doubt, is essential for successful performance; but any careful reader who is prepared to spend the necessary time should be able to master, without difficulty, the basic principles of self-defence as expounded in this book.

I wish this publication all success.

Alan Rose

Colombo.

CONTENTS

Foreword	5
Precepts	11
Preface	13
Introduction	17
Explanation of Illustrations	27

CHAPTER ONE
Defensive and offensive postures	31

CHAPTER TWO
Defences against a hand-squeeze from front and holds from behind

Defence No. 1.	Hand-shake lock	34

Defences against holds from behind

Defence No. 2.	Flying mare	37
	A ground-lock	37
,, No. 3.	The right elbow-dig	38
,, No. 4.	A squat-on-knee breaker	39
	Ground-locks	40
,, No. 5.	A "back-heel" scrotum kick	41

CHAPTER THREE

Defences against grips on waist		42
Defence No. 1.	Armpit collar-bone grip	42
,, No. 2.	Head-to-foot twist	43
,, No. 3.	An elbow break	43

CONTENTS

Defence No. 4.	Double nerve-centre pinch and come-along hold	44
,, No. 5.	Elbow-break and throw	46
,, No. 6.	Forelock-hold, arm-lock	46
	Additional defences	47

Defences against a push-on-the-chest

Defence No. 7.	"Spine-breaker"	47

Defences against arm-holds or pulls

Defence No. 8.	The "snake-coil grip" and arm-lock	48
,, No. 9.	Single-handed arm twist or snake-coil grip	50

Defence against blindfolding from behind

Defence No. 10.	A blindfold shoulder throw	51

CHAPTER FOUR

Defences against kicks		53
Defence No. 1.	A leg-hold turn-over throw	53
,, No. 2.	Ankle-hold knee-breaker	54

CHAPTER FIVE

Defences against club or pole attacks		56
Defence No. 1.	Arms-twist and stomach-blow	57
,, No. 2.	Arms-twist rod-end dig	58

Defence with a walking-stick

Defence No. 3.	A dig at temple	58

CONTENTS

Defence No. 4.		A leg-trip and push Additional defences Scrotum-blow or knee-break	59 59

Defences against club attacks

Defence No. 5.		An arm-lock	59
,,	No. 6.	A hand-twist and dig-at-rib	60

CHAPTER SIX

Defences against knife or dagger attacks			62
Defence No. 1.		Straight-arm elbow-break	63
,,	No. 2.	Bent-arm lock	64
,,	No. 3.	Standing-leg lock or knee-break	64
,,	No. 4.	A shoulder-throw	65
,,	No. 5.	A hip-throw A ground-lock	65 66
,,	No. 6.	Crotch-hold roll-over-shoulders throw	66
,,	No. 7.	Roll-over-back throw	67
,,	No. 8.	Nape-hold somersault throw A ground-lock	67 68
,,	No. 9.	Wrist-and-cheek hold leg-trip	68
,,	No. 10.	Wrist-and-sleeve hold knee-trip A ground-lock	69 69
,,	No. 11.	Throw-at-eyes revolving knee-kick	70
,,	No. 12.	Double-foot knee-breaker	71
,,	No. 13.	A knife-dropping stomach-cut	71
,,	No. 14.	A jugular-press and arm-trap	72

CONTENTS

Defence No. 15.	Wrist-pull and hip-kick	73
,, No. 16.	Wrist-pull and trip	74
,, No. 17.	A wrist-parry knee-kick	75
,, No. 18.	A knife-dropping nerve-cut	75
,, No. 19.	Arm-break hip-throw	76
,, No. 20.	Hand-twist and dig	76

Defences against knife attacks with a walking-stick

Defence No. 21.	Wrist-parry elbow-blow	77
,, No. 22.	Hand-twist and stick-dig	77

Two v. One

Defence No. 23.	Hand-twist and elbow-dig	78
,, No. 24.	Neck-twist and knee-kick	79
	Additional defences	80

CHAPTER SEVEN

Defences against pistol or revolver attacks		81
Defence No. 1.	Wrist-grip and throat-axe	82
,, No. 2.	Bent-arm wrist-breaker	82
,, No. 3.	Wrist-hold, trip-and-push	83
,, No. 4.	Double-arm-twist arm-lock	83

Charts showing secret nerve-centres and vital spots, explaining their actions and reactions

Chart I	85
Chart II	88

IMPORTANT—TEN PRECEPTS

Every student of this Unarmed Combat must observe the following ten precepts at all times.

Remember (1) Whilst practising with a partner that locks, holds, throws and kicks can be injurious to the person practised upon.

(2) Not to use more force or pressure than is necessary in the application of locks, holds, etc., and not to practise with one who delights in exhibiting his strength.

(3) To begin with slow motion, step by step, and practise until the complete defence can be performed in one continuous movement.

(4) That "practice makes perfect". Practise therefore every defence as often as possible.

(5) To use a rubber dagger at the start whilst practising the defences against dagger (knife)

attacks, and an actual steel dagger after gaining experience to remove the natural fear.

(6) To control your temper, and never to apply pressure on vital spots in anger.

(7) Not to attack anyone first, and always to avoid heated arguments.

(8) Not to use this Art for any evil purpose or with any evil motive to bring dishonour on this Noble Art, and not to hesitate to resort to it to safeguard your life and property or the honour of a woman.

(9) That this Art is primarily intended to suppress crime and lawlessness of all sorts.

(10) To perform the "Guru Salute" before practising the defences, once daily.

PREFACE

As a result of World War II there has been a continuous and rapid increase in thefts, hold-ups, highway robberies, molestation of women, assaults on law-abiding citizens and various other nefarious activities of the lawless, all over the world, particularly in Ceylon.

I attribute the increase in these high-handed activities mainly to the average man's ignorance of the art of self-defence. The need of the art of unarmed combat was never more felt at any age than it is today. In these circumstances I have acceded to the numerous requests of my pupils and the admirers of the art to publish some powerful and simplified defences which could easily be mastered by all law-abiding citizens.

My eclectic system of "cheena-adi cum jujutsu" self-defence was devised and developed after twelve years of silent research. In publishing this system of unarmed combat for the first time, I have eliminated the superfluous, exhibition and the sporting sections of both cheena-adi and jujutsu. This system is therefore the best that the combined art could impart to the average peace-loving citizen.

My technique is based mainly on the art of cheena-adi, coupled with the esoteric branch of ju-jutsu, i.e. the self-defence portion of ju-jutsu, wrestling and the Indian art of stick-defence. These defences are in their most refined modern forms and this volume should meet with every requirement of the average educated person.

The preparation of this book has taken over three years. Every lock, every throw and every type of attack, defence and defensive-offence given in this volume has been proved flawless. Whilst promoting all-round physical development, these defences bring no adverse effects to any part of the body. Ladies can practise these without any ill-effects except, of course, during the period of pregnancy. I would commend this art to every female, as there has been a marked increase in molestation in the recent past with the narrowing down of the difference of sex in politics, social service and employment. All young educated people should be encouraged to learn the art of self-defence as this is the only art in the world that teaches "self-control" both in theory and practice. It reforms a hot-tempered man into a sober and cool-headed person. Japanese consider the man who loses his temper to be one who is mentally not sound. It is absolutely erroneous to suppose that a knowledge of the art of self-defence will instil an excessive degree of the "fighting spirit" into members of the younger generation.

One who has mastered my technique of unarmed combat explained in this volume, should be able to multiply them (like permutation and combination) into several more effective defences and defensive-offences.

It should be the motto of every student of this art to put down crime and assist the authorities in weeding out lawlessness in every country. Lawlessness and crime of any sort in any country must necessarily diminish with the spread of this most scientific art of unarmed combat (viz. : cheena-adi cum ju-jutsu self-defence) yet devised.

My sincere gratitude is due to my "Guru", the late Mr. Richard Peries of Kotahena, Colombo, my pupil-colleague, Mr. N. I. V. Fernando, of the Telegraph Department, and my friend and pupil, Mr. W. Gunapala, of the Ceylon Government Railway.

The late Mr. Richard Peries was one of the best exponents of the arts of cheena-adi, ju-jutsu, sword-play and stick defence, Ceylon had ever produced. Just as a duckling takes to water Mr. Richard Peries's taste for these arts was inborn. His father, Mr. Haramanis Peries, who predeceased him, was also an expert in cheena-adi self-defence during his lifetime.

R. A. Vairamuttu

INTRODUCTION

Ju-jutsu is supposed to have been practised in Japan for over 2,000 years, and cheena-adi or China-footing, the Chinese art of unarmed attack and defence—the older of the two arts—can be traced to the mythological age. Both these arts have been jealously guarded secrets for many centuries, and imparted only to well-disciplined pupils of sound moral character.

To the Gods Kadori and Kashima the Japanese trace the origin of ju-jutsu and believe that the secrets of this art were revealed to the Samurai (the warrior caste) who maintained law and order in the kingdom of Japan.

Though the Chinese art of unarmed combat is scientifically the best by test, yet nothing is known about its founder. This art started on its decline with the disintegration of the Celestial Empire of China about the fifteenth century. But just as no secret can always remain a secret, so this system made secret access to Korea, Japan, Java and Ceylon. There is no doubt that the Ceylonese and Javanese have preserved this art in its pristine purity.

It is believed that, during the Ming Dynasty, some Japanese went to China to learn their closely guarded art. CHUEN YUAN PIN or CHIN GEN PIN of the Chinese Ming Dynasty went to Japan and taught the art to the Japanese. Akiyama Shirobie Yoshitoki, a physician of Nagasaki, Japan, founder of a "RYUGI" (Institution) known as "YOSHIN-RYU" had learnt the Chinese art under a Chinese teacher named HAKU-TEI or PAO-CHUAN in China, according to *The Art of Ju-jutsu* by E. J. Harrison. The present high standard of ju-jutsu in Japan is entirely due to the introduction of the Chinese art into their system by the few medical men of Japan who studied both these arts.

During the reign of King Vijaya Bahu VI, a Chinese eunuch named CHIN-HO was sent to Ceylon by the Chinese Emperor YUNG-HO of the Ming Dynasty in the year 1405 to bring the "DALADA", the sacred Tooth Relic of the Lord Gautama Buddha.

As his mission was a failure he went back to China and returned to Ceylon in the year 1410. In memory of his visit to Ceylon, a carved stone inscribed in Chinese, Tamil and Persian characters was erected in 1409. A British engineer named H. F. Tomalin, who was employed in Ceylon, happened to discover in 1911 that slab of stone with inscription at Galle, the capital of the southern province of this beautiful isle. The eunuch CHIN-HO and his followers were believed to be adepts in their art of unarmed combat.

INTRODUCTION

China's ancient literature has many references to Ceylon. There are genuine records of pilgrimages of Buddhists from China to Ceylon since the third century. The famous Chinese explorer Fa Hien came on pilgrimage to Ceylon in the early fifth century and visited the holy places of Buddhism and spent two years in making copies of Buddhist scriptures. There were constant cultural and commercial relations between China and Ceylon for several hundreds of years from the third century. The first Ceylon Embassy in China was established during the early fifth century about A.D. 410. Several hundreds of Chinese coins of the Tang dynasty from the seventh century up to the Sung dynasty of the thirteenth century have been unearthed in many parts of Ceylon at different times.

Although it is believed that the Chinese art of unarmed combat was first introduced into Japan during the Ming dynasty in the fourteenth century, this art found its way into Ceylon hundreds of years earlier. But the art was not widely imparted to one and all. The majority of the pupils had to be satisfied with only a superficial knowledge. As none of the teachers imparted all the "secrets" to any pupil, general enthusiasm gradually faded. Even today it is the same old story with any cheena-adi Guru. If anyone ardently desires to master the advanced secrets of the art, one has to learn from as many experts as possible and by continuing to learn right through. With every successive master one undergoes training, one has to pretend to be a complete novice without exhibiting the knowledge gained from the previous teacher or teachers. Thus I have mastered this art and ju-jutsu self-defence, and ventured to publish this book for the benefit of educated and law-abiding citizens.

The two arts which were on the decline, primarily owing to secrecy and also to the limited number of persons to whom the knowledge was imparted, had a complete revival during the fourteenth century.

Ju-jutsu developed into various distinct schools under different teachers, but the revival of the Chinese art was only short-lived and began to decline further and further after the fifteenth century.

Ju-jutsu continued to flourish during and after the lifetime of Professor Jigoro Kano. Dr. Kano founded the Kano system of ju-jutsu named judo. His system of judo was recognized by the Japanese Government and adopted by the Army, Navy and the Police Departments, in all universities and higher institutions. Every educated male and female in Japan learned ju-jutsu and it is included in the curriculum of all educational institutions.

Judo (ju-jutsu) won the admiration of the Occidentals in view of its efficacy through simplicity. It was introduced into Great Britain for the first time by Professor Yukio Tani and Raku Uyenishi between 1895 and 1899, according to E. J. Harrison in *The Art of Ju-jutsu*.

The first amateur society of judo named the BUDOKWAI was founded in London by G. KOIZUMI more than thirty years ago, and its first instructor was YUKIO TANI. The Japanese Ambassadors have always been elected as the Honorary Presidents up to the time of World War II. The BUDOKWAI is affiliated to the KODOKWAN, TOKYO, founded by Dr. Jigoro Kano of Japan. Now the art of judo (ju-jutsu) is extensively practised in Britain, Canada, U.S.A., France and South Africa and introduced into their Navy, Army, Air Force and Police Departments. Women in the war services have been trained in ju-jutsu. Women in the Western countries have taken a keen interest in the art. America has taken a keener interest in ju-jutsu than any other country in the world barring Japan. Whether the real secrets of advanced ju-jutsu, which are so greatly treasured by the Japanese and imparted under vow of strict secrecy to pupils of unquestionable moral character, have ever been divulged to Occidentals, is very much open to doubt.

The Eastern arts of unarmed combat are undoubtedly superior to the present-day Western arts of self-defences. The principal systems of combat and sporting arts in the East and the West can be tabulated as follows :—

EASTERN

1. Judo (or ju-jutsu) of the Japanese. The art of gentleness, or the soft art.
2. Kempo or Kenjutsu of the Japanese. The hard art or the art of defence against armed assailants or sudden attacks.
3. Roku-Shaku-Bo or Han-bo (stick defence) of the Japanese.
4. Sumo or wrestling of the Japanese.
5. Cheena-adi of the Chinese. The most scientific art of self-defence against assailants armed or not.
6. Gusthi (wrestling) of the Indians. A sporting combat.
7. Lathie or stick defence of the Indians. A self-defence art against several assailants.
8. Sword display of the Indians.

WESTERN

1. Boxing (originated in Athens by Theseus, son of Aegeus, King of Athens).
2. Fencing of the French.
3. Wrestling which is further divided into—
   (a) amateur wrestling,
   (b) catch-as-catch-can wrestling,
   (c) Cumberland and Westmorland wrestling,

(d) Graeco-Roman wrestling,
(e) all-in wrestling.
4. La Savate (foot-fighting)—a French sport.
5. Shillelagh or cudgel play. Irish.

Combined Arts—
1. *Pancration* is an old form of Greek physical contest which is a combination of boxing and wrestling.
2. *Siamese Boxing*. In boxing contests in Siam kicking is also allowed.

Although boxing is today considered to be a Western art its origin has been traced to Athens round about 900 B.C. It is the third oldest sporting combat of the world and competitors then fought with bare fists seated face to face. It was a cruel sport as both contestants bled profusely. This form of sport spread into Greece and later Romans adopted and reformed it.

Foot-racing is considered to be the oldest form of sport with wrestling as the second oldest in the world. But Indian Gusthi (wrestling) and Lathie (stick) defence could be traced many thousands of years back to the mythological age. The Lathie defence is also one of the most scientific arts of self-defence against several, performed with systematic and rhythmical movements of feet and hands whilst the blows are delivered with the end and tip at vital spots of the opponents.

Ju-jutsu can be divided into three categories and to be an exponent of this art, a thorough knowledge of the three sections must be mastered.

1. *Wrestling portion of ju-jutsu*

    This section teaches only the sporting and exhibition part of the art. This is again subdivided into two branches:

    (a) *Nage-Waza*—which deals with the primary tricks of pulling and pushing, tripping and other tricks of breaking the balance of the opponent.

    (b) *Katame-Waza*—which deals with the art of holding down an opponent by means of locks, holds, etc.

2. *The Atemi-Waza* or esoteric self-defence division of ju-jutsu

    This deals with effective knock-out blows dealt at vital spots whether opponents are armed or otherwise. This section comprises cuts with edge of palms, digs with fingers or elbows and kicking and hitting with legs and hands respectively on vital spots. This portion is taught only under a vow of secrecy to selected pupils of sound moral character.

3. *Katsu or Resuscitation*
   This section of advanced secrets of jujutsu deals with the art of resuscitation or revival after the delivery of fatal blows on opponents. This section also teaches a unique art of resuscitation from the after effects of falls, strangulations, drowning, etc. Katsu should be administered immediately after the fatal blows, drowning or strangulation. This is taught to a fewer number of far advanced pupils of unstained moral character under a vow of strictest secrecy.

The Technique—The fundamental principles in this unarmed combat are based on balance, leverage, spring-action, momentum and gravitation. This is an art in which the movement, force, weight, height, clothing and even the hair on the head of one's opponent is used to his disadvantage.

Balance is of supreme importance for any form of physical exertion. Gravity is the force with which we are attracted to the earth, and the centre of gravity of any object or person in the normal course should fall within the base. The moment an object or person is slanted or tilted the centre of gravity falls outside the base and the object or person must necessarily topple unless there be other support or cause to regain the balance. The systematic and rhythmic movements of the feet in cheena-adi is to retain unshakable balance at all times, besides attack and defence.

Leverage movements are important for easy lifting and throwing and for application of locks and holds with the least effort and energy.

The vital spots of the human body to which cuts, digs, blows and kicks are delivered, and the nerve centres which are pinched, or digs and cuts administered, must be very carefully studied by every student of unarmed combat. It will thus be seen that this scientific art has been devised with great skill by master-minds with good knowledge of human anatomy, science, philosophy and all important aspects of life. SELF-DEFENCE and SELF-CONTROL bring SELF-RESPECT.

In the lessons which follow I have explained in pictures and notes some of the principal defences selected from cheena-adi, ju-jutsu, wrestling and stick defences combined, to meet the requirements of anyone who desires to master this system of unarmed combat.

Anyone who wants to learn the more advanced and intricate defences in this technique and the complete art of cheena-adi can communicate with me. Such enthusiasts shall always receive my prompt attention and ready co-operation.

R. A. Vairamuttu

P. O. Box 1063,
   Colombo,
      Ceylon.

EXPLANATION OF ILLUSTRATIONS

Illustration 1

The author twenty-two years back. Still maintains a sound physique.

Illustrations 2-3

This shows the author's everlasting zeal in physical culture.

Fifteen minutes daily allotted to any form of "approved" physical exercises would definitely help one to possess a "Healthy Mind in a Healthy Body".

Illustrations 2 to 9 are included to show the keen interest the author has in physical culture. Physical culture is not meant for a particular age but for a lifetime. The author is a life member of the "Health and Strength League" of Great Britain, the objects of which are :—

"To bind together in a bond of robust brotherhood, all physical culturists and athletes throughout the world. A bond united for the purpose of disseminating the broad principles of, and in nature's way promoting the cause of health and strength," should receive the serious consideration of every enthusiast of self-defence.

Illustrations 4-7

These pictures were taken very recently. Indian clubs, skipping rope, spring grips and free-hand exercises have helped the author to maintain a robust physique throughout for a period of over twenty-five years.

PHYSICAL CULTURE IN RELATION TO THE ART OF SELF-DEFENCE

The art of self-defence explained in the forthcoming chapters is primarily intended for the weak against the "mighty". But no one is born to be a weakling in this world. Negligence of physical exercise, healthy habits, and vicious negative thinking make them so.

Is it not a crying shame to move in society in a dilapidated, sickly state of health with worn-out, under-developed and stunted muscles making one look very much older than one's age? They are looked down upon by society and they never attract the admiration of the fair sex. They are pitied even by the fair sex who have now taken up physical culture, wrestling and ju-jutsu.

The art of self-defence encourages everyone to maintain good health in order that they can keep fit to face eventualities. There is no other royal road, there is no better patent, than physical exercise to promote a healthy nervous and muscular system. Physical exercises stimulate the entire body, increase and purify the blood supply and produce an abundance of vim, vigour and vitality.

Exercises, in addition to cleansing the waste matter of the muscles, remove the poison that gets into the blood supply. Physical exercises, whilst developing and strengthening the muscles, tone up the growth of bones and the function of respiration.

The value of exercises is emphasized as this is the unique system of producing radiant health, energy and vitality, whilst giving a medicinal toning effect to cure constipation, obesity and nervous disorders. Lessons in cheena-adi—this ancient Asian unarmed combat—are a splendid course of exercises which promote all-round physical development. The other most easily accessible exercises that produce amazingly quick all-round development are walking, swimming, skipping and Indian club-swinging. Horse riding is also one of the most splendid all-round exercises though not easily accessible to all.

Illustration 8

Dipping exercises are some of the most valuable exercises for developing the arms and the upper part of the body.

This exercise is not performed with the palms placed flat on the ground, but with the weight of the whole body resting on thumb and first two fingers and toes. Strong fingers are an asset to this art of self-defence.

Illustration 9

This is one of the most effective balancing exercises that help in the maintenance of correct poise in the self-defence feats.

Guru Salute

The fine art of self-defence has, just as any of the religious doctrines or scientific inventions, its founder, though unknown. All teachers and students of this art pay homage and reverence to the original "Guru", that unknown founder of this wonderful art, by a formal salutation immediately before the performance of any of these feats. Some teachers go a step further and insist that failure to perform the "Guru" salute would develop in them a tendency to misuse the art.

Illustration (10) shows the author (on the left) and his pupils observing the "Guru" salute known in cheena-adi as "Guru-Namaskar".

Study illustration (10) carefully and never fail to observe the "Guru Salute" daily before the other lessons are attempted.

CHAPTER ONE

DEFENSIVE AND OFFENSIVE POSTURES

This lesson deals with the foot-work of the first steps in cheena-adi. The purpose of foot-work is to give correct and easy movements in a struggle. Whilst practising these you will observe that they are designed to stress the importance of balance. You must be in a position to move, side-step, advance, or back-step with perfect ease and maintaining perfect balance *at all times*. Unlike ju-jutsu where balance helps to defend, the poses in cheena-adi, whilst giving you unshakeable balance, also serve as your best offensive positions.

Illustration (11) shows the normal posture. The four circles which are about 27 inches apart are for the guidance of movements. *See* illustration (12). This is the first forward movement. Side-step to circle No. (1) with your right foot and take your left foot forward to circle No. (4), left knee slightly bent. As the left foot is taken forward the right foot should be turned out so that it is at right-angles to the left. You will notice that you are perfectly at ease in this posture. This is a forward left self-defensive posture.

Illustration (13) shows arms stiffened with fists closed and ready for action, is both an offensive and a defensive position.

Illustration (14) shows the side-step to the left. Bring your left foot from circle (4) to circle (2) whilst turning the right foot at circle (1) to right-angles with the left. This posture is also both offensive and defensive. Left hand to defend and the right to give a two-finger dig.

Illustration (15) shows the side movement to the right. This is done by bringing the right foot from circle (1) to (3). You will notice that the left foot though unmoved is still at right-angles to the right. Notice also that the bent left knee straightens as the right knee is bent in changing position from illustration (14) to (15). This is a forward right self-defensive posture.

Illustration (16) shows defensive position from which you can attack in two directions—front and to your right either with your right hand or right leg.

A forward offensive and defensive posture is shown in illustration 17.

Illustration 18 shows a side-defensive posture and illustration 19 a side or forward offensive posture. Note how in illustration 19 the right hand is ready to deliver a deadly cut.

Illustration 12 is the reverse of this posture from which a left-hand cut can be delivered. Similarly illustration 13 is the reverse of 16.

Mark four circles on a spacious floor and practise these movements in all directions until you get used to these movements with perfect ease. The important feature is to see that one foot is at right-angles to the other, and the knee of the leg that is in front is always bent while the other leg is straight. Movement of one foot and turning of the other at right-angles should be done simultaneously.

This lesson may appear to be rather difficult and tedious at first sight but nevertheless it must be thoroughly mastered.

Refer to illustrations 94 to 97 and see how a favourite revolving knee-kick can be administered from the position in illustration 14. Instead of turning at 90 degrees here you revolve on the ball of your left foot at 180 degrees, and a most effective knee-kick can be delivered with perfect ease. By revolving 180 degrees in the opposite direction from the same illustration (14) on the same foot, you can give an instep kick at the scrotum, ribs or at the abdomen.

CHAPTER TWO

DEFENCES AGAINST A "HAND-SQUEEZE" FROM FRONT AND "HOLDS" FROM BEHIND

Defence 1

Hand-Shake Lock

Some people at times take a great delight in exhibiting their amazing strength by a tight grip or a hard squeeze, whilst in a supposed friendly hand-shake. If you happen to be the victim of such a vicious hand-shake, you will no doubt be placed in an embarrassing position, particularly so, if it occurs in the presence of your friends or ladies, when you are not his physical equal to resist or retaliate, especially when he makes you rise on your toes wriggling with pain.

A bully may try this on you through his rowdy mentality coupled with an air of physical superiority, in order to tease or belittle you in the presence of his or your friends.

The art of self-defence is the only medium (a friend-in-need) through which you could not only free yourself instantaneously from such a situation, but also teach the opponent a good lesson as to how his strength succumbs to this art.

Illustration (20) shows how an opponent (in T-shirt) has secured a tight grip and is squeezing your hand. You are taken somewhat unawares. The first thing that should strike your mind is the self-defensive posture, by placing the right foot forward, the knee slightly bent, and the feet at right-angles to each other (*see* illustration 20).

Now shift the position of your right foot from the self-defensive posture by taking a step towards his right as in illustration (21) in a right-angular movement, whilst gripping your opponent's palm held down tightly with downward pressure, at the same time taking a swift leftward turn of the body (*see* illustrations 21 and 22). Whilst taking the leftward turn bring your left leg with a swing and place it behind or near your opponent's right foot as in illustration (22), still maintaining the grip of your opponent's hand which gets twisted and bent at the wrist and elbow by this time, as in illustration (22).

Your opponent's hand gets locked and he will be helpless in this position. Even a gentle twist of his hand would make him arch backwards as in illustration (23) and yell with unbearable pain, which runs from his wrist right down his arm, spine and legs to his toes.

If you do not wish your opponent to suffer from a backward fall causing serious injuries, keep your left thigh just behind your opponent's right thigh, and hold the back of his neck with your left open palm, thus making him realize his folly, when every inch of his body aches with excruciating pain.

The whole operation from the start of handshake until completion of the "lock" is one continuous movement performed in a flash.

Just visualize within yourself the haughty and arrogant attitude your opponent adopted when he squeezed your hand (illustration 20), and the predicament in which he is placed the very next moment (illustration 23), brought about by the simple process of turning and twisting, with systematic movement of feet performed with little effort.

Warning

Whilst practising with a partner perform every move slowly, step by step, being in readiness to stop short on hearing the word "stop" from the partner, when he cannot bear the pain any longer. You will gain speed gradually with constant practice.

Never practise these locks and defences with one who delights in exhibiting his strength or prowess, to avoid disastrous consequences. Once you have grasped the "technique" of this art and its underlying principles, you will be in a position to know (whilst practising these locks, holds, grips, etc.) when and where to stop at the "hurting point" without causing any injury to your partner.

Defences for "Holds from Behind"

Defence 2

Flying Mare

Illustration (24) speaks for itself the position you are placed in, when you are caught from behind, around your arms, unawares. Remember in such a situation to keep a cool head and to act swiftly. Bending and lowering your body slightly, step forward, raise with a jerk your hands upwards and sideways, bent at the elbows at right-angles to the forearms as in (25). This action will loosen your arms from his hold. Now, with your hands, grip your opponent's right wrist and straighten his arm over your right shoulder with a sudden pull, bringing him close against your back, as in illustration (26), and throw him forward, as in illustration (27). This throw is popularly known as the "flying mare". Now proceed with the ground lock, as in illustration (28), as a further punishment if you so desire.

Ground-Lock

When your opponent is thrown on the ground, still maintaining the grip at his right wrist, go down on your left leg to a squatting position, bringing your right leg and crossing it over his arm, encircling same, so that his forearm falls on your calf.

Now turn his palm upwards as in illustration (28). His arm can now be dislocated both at the shoulder and at the elbow joints. With your free right hand you can deliver a cut at the Adam's apple, jugular vein, or solar-plexus.

NOTE: Stop at the position in illustration (27) whilst practising.

Defence 3

THE RIGHT ELBOW-DIG

From position in illustration 24, place your right leg forward as before and relinquishing the grip as in illustration (25), twist your body towards the left, as in illustration (29). Keep your opponent's arms still raised, and give a "back-hand" dig at his solar-plexus with your right elbow, as in illustration (30). All the moves should be done in a flash.

Reverse the process to give the left elbow dig.

Warning

Whilst practising never give the dig to your partner, as this is one of the most fatal digs known to this art of self-defence.

SCIENTIFIC UNARMED COMBAT 39

Defence 4

A Squat-on-Knee Breaker

From position in illustration (24), move one of your legs sideways, bearing in mind that if your right leg is moved, you can grip your opponent's right ankle as in illustration (31) or vice versa. Raising both your hands up as in illustration (25), bend down in a flash with hands thrust downwards and gripping your opponent's ankle quickly raise his leg with a sudden jerk. Whilst bending down to grip his ankle give him a push with your buttocks. Rest your buttocks on his knee while maintaining the upward pull at the ankle as in illustration (32). Your opponent must then fall with a bruised leg. Further injuries may be caused by your falling on his abdomen or the back of his head coming in violent contact against a hard object or hard ground.

Ground-Lock

Illustration 33

Immediately your opponent falls on his back, revolve to the right on the ball of your left foot, and as you do so bring your right leg across with a swing and place the sole of your right (shoe) foot at the left thigh of your opponent. At the same time, trapping his ankle in your right armpit, go down to the position seen in illustration (33). Bring your left forearm under his calf and pull his entrapped right foot behind with your back, whilst pushing hard with your foot at the inner thigh in a splitting manner. Unbearable pain will be caused to every inch of his body but felt badly at his hip joints and spinal column.

Illustration (34) is a variation where the right foot is placed at his left ankle and his right ankle is grasped with the left palm and pushed farther away to bring about the same effect.

Ground-Locks
(applied after throws)

Illustration 35

Holding his right wrist go down to the squatting position on your left leg, whilst shooting your right leg under his right arm and place same on his chest. Place the other hand on his cheek and apply pressure both at his cheek and at the wrist, palm turned up, using the leg as fulcrum.

This would cause dislocation of the elbow.

Illustration (36) shows a variation where you go down on your right knee and use the thigh bone as fulcrum.

Defence 5

A "Back-Heel" Scrotum Kick

In case your opponent referred to in previous defences happens to be a tall and an extraordinarily strong man, he might sometimes raise you above ground with his hold around your arms. You will notice that none of the defences explained earlier could then be applied. As your opponent lifts you above ground, allow him to do so at ease, or even just assist him in the act by jerking yourself up (as in a high jump), and when you are being lifted up give a sharp back-heel kick at his scrotum.

Warning

Be extremely careful not to kick at the scrotum whilst practising.

CHAPTER THREE

DEFENCES AGAINST GRIPS AT WAIST

If an opponent gets a firm grip at your trouser band or any clothing you wear, from the front, as in illustration (37), with his right hand, there are various tricks or counter grips, nerve pinches, digs, etc., to make him release the grip instantaneously. There are also many locks by the application of which his arm could be broken or dislocated at the wrist, elbow or shoulder.

Defence 1

ARMPIT COLLAR-BONE GRIP

Step forward with your right leg, thrust your right hand at his right shoulder and obtain a firm grip with your thumb and first finger, digging your thumb under the armpit and your first (index) finger into the hollow behind the collar-bone, as in illustration (38).

This vice-like grip makes his right arm or even his whole body paralysed.

If your opponent holds you with his left hand apply the grip with your left hand.

SCIENTIFIC UNARMED COMBAT

Warning

Be very careful, whilst practising, not to pull with this grip on, as the collar-bone will get dislocated.

Defence 2

Head-to-Foot Twist

From position in illustration (37) thrust both your hands forward placing the hollow of your right palm against your opponent's chin and gripping his hair on the back of his head with your left hand, give a sudden twist to his left side, pushing with your right and pulling with your left, as in illustration (39). This will result in your opponent getting twisted from head to foot and falling on the ground.

You may then apply any of the ground-locks.

If your opponent happens to be one with a specially developed strong neck (as that of all-in wrestlers) place your right leg behind his right leg and trip him whilst twisting his head sideways.

Defence 3

An Elbow Break

From position in illustration (37) hold his wrist with your right hand and give a sharp tap with the little finger side of the clenched fist or the heel of your left palm at his elbow. This will dislocate his right elbow.

Defence 4

DOUBLE NERVE-CENTRE PINCH AND COME-ALONG HOLD

At this stage it will benefit you to understand the varying degrees of pain brought about by a normal pinch, a nerve pinch and a nerve-centre pinch. A knowledge of human anatomy is essential to understand properly the positions of the nerves and nerve-centres.

Pinch your own body and note the differences of pain when you pinch at the nerve-centres explained in the defences that follow. The strongest man can be made motionless with these nerve-centre pinches.

On the nerves and nerve-centres which cannot be pinched, you can administer cuts, blows, digs and kicks. The cuts and blows of course are not limited to nerve-centres, but can be delivered on all other vital spots.

From illustration (37) you can apply this double nerve-centre pinch as shown in illustration (40).

Pinch at your opponent's fleshy space between the thumb and the first finger with your right thumb and first finger, thumb placed above and the first finger underneath (both fingers held as the claws of a vice). At the same time, pinch with your left thumb on the nerve-centre at the elbow joint placing the other fingers underneath. You can locate these two spots by pinching your own hand. Where the pain is most severe when pinched are the identical spots. (*See* 13 and 14 in chart I, page 85).

If you pinch at these exact spots correctly your opponent will release his grip immediately, as one removes his hand when pricked with a pin.

With the pressure of the pinch at the elbow still maintained, slide your right palm over his hand and bend down his wrist at right-angles to the forearm, as in illustration (41). Move towards him bringing his forearm against your body. Releasing the elbow-pinch, whilst maintaining the downward pressure at the wrist to prevent his arm being straightened, slide your left forearm round his elbow, so that the back of his elbow falls into the crook of your left elbow, as in illustration (42). Now you will notice that your forearm is at right-angles to your upper arm and the two forearms come into line. Open the fingers of your right hand and place your left palm on his downward bent hand (a process of transferring the pressure at the wrist from one hand to the other). After securing a firm grip with your left hand you can take off your right hand, as in illustration (42). This is one of the finest come-along holds.

Warning

Warning

Whilst practising never use more pressure than is necessary as you might damage your opponent's wrist.

Defence 5

ELBOW-BREAK AND THROW

From position in illustration (40) with the two nerve pinches, bring his hand to the position in illustration (43). Raise your opponent's arm and step forward with the left foot, wheeling to the right on the ball of your left foot, bring his straightened arm over your left shoulder as in illustration (44). You can now break his arm at the elbow (using shoulder as the fulcrum) by applying downward the pressure at the wrist, or draw him close against your body and throw him forward. Proceed with a ground-lock if required (*See* Ill. 28, 35, 36 and 80).

Defence 6

FORELOCK-HOLD, ARM-LOCK

If your opponent grips your forelock as in illustration (45) with his right hand, place the little-finger-edge side of your left forearm against his forearm about 2 inches from his wrist towards the elbow (palm facing him), and bring your right arm up from underneath enclosing his forearm, and interlock the fingers as shown in illustration (46); and with a scissors-motion, force his hand down and away from you. This causes his arm to be bent at the elbow and gets locked as in illustration (47) causing unbearable pain.

Warning

Continued downward pressure would dislocate the shoulder joint. Be extremely careful whilst practising.

Additional Defences

You can apply the "collar-bone armpit hold" described in illustration (38) or administer the two-finger dig at the solar plexus.

Defence 7

Defences Against a Push-on-the-Chest

A "Spine-Breaker"

If an opponent attempts to push or pushes you as in illustration (48), strike his hand off with your clenched left fist in an up and outward motion.

Shoot both your arms straight through alongside his waist (between his arms and the body), and lock your fingers in a chain-grip at his small-of-the-back, so that the left knuckles come in contact with his spine. At the same time, butting at the centre of his chest with your head, draw him in with your chain-gripped hands as in illustration (49), and give a sharp pin-point pressure with your protruding left-centre knuckle. This will make your opponent suddenly flop and bend into an "S". You can now drop him to fall flat on his back by the mere separation of your gripped hands and simultaneously pushing with your head.

Warning

Be extremely careful whilst practising as the application of too much pressure would result in the breakage of his spine.

DEFENCES FOR ARM-HOLDS OR PULLS

Defence 8

THE "SNAKE-COIL GRIP" AND ARM-LOCK

If a bully or rowdy pulls your left arm with his left hand, and if you happen to be the weaker, you are very likely to be tumbled down and "lick the dust". Here again this art will aid you to turn the tables on the opponent to apply an effortless "arm-

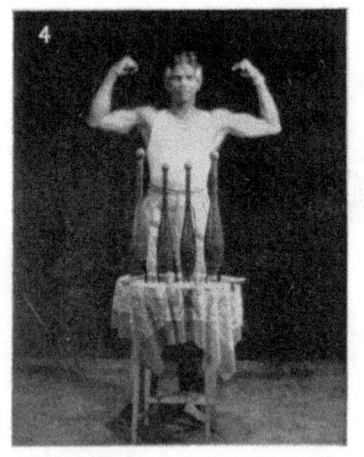

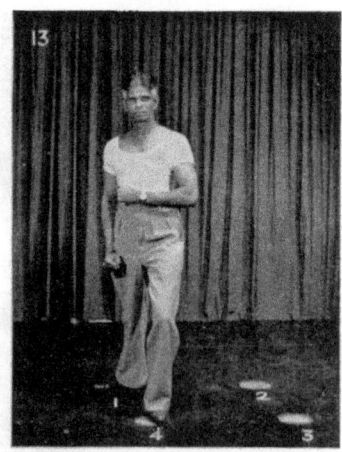

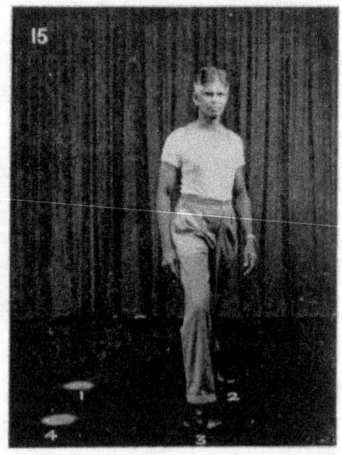

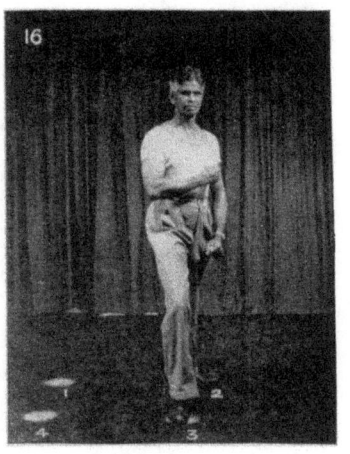

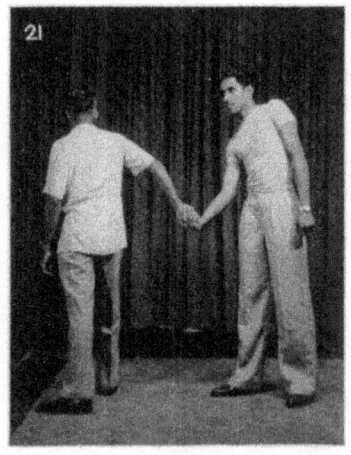
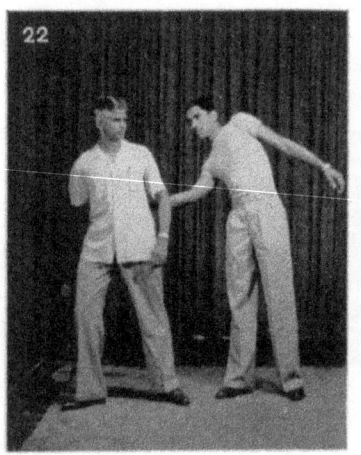

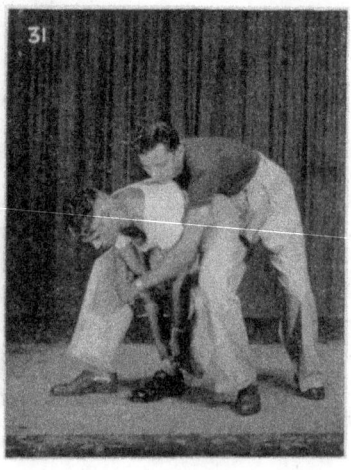

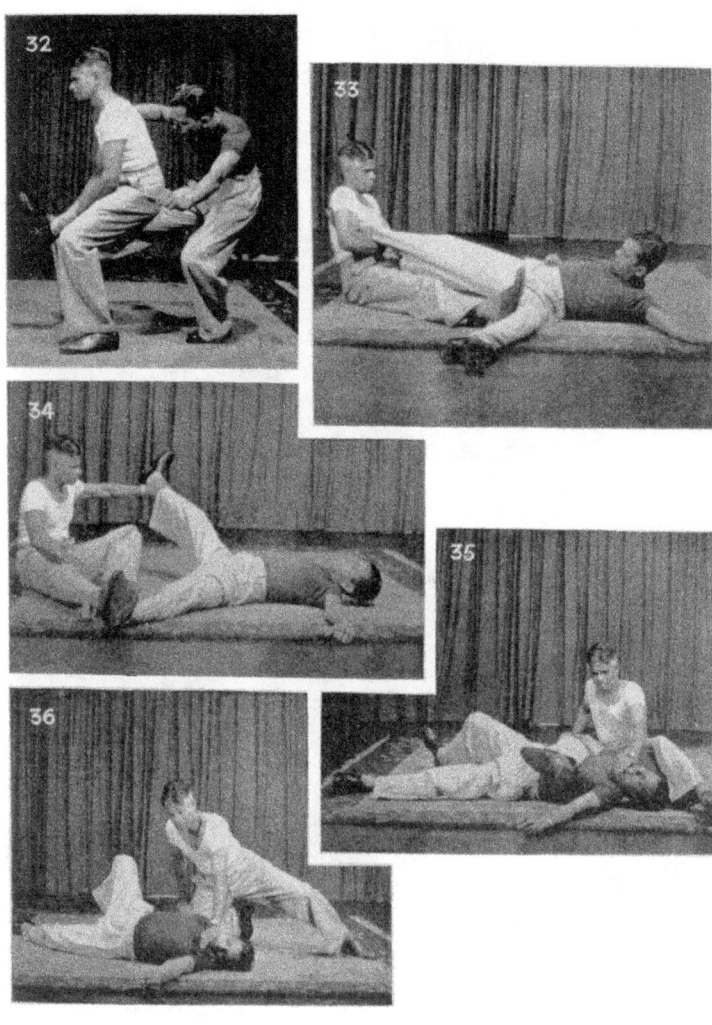

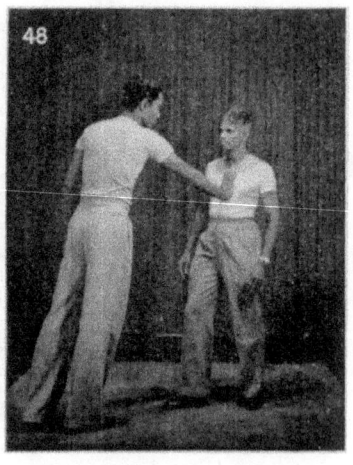

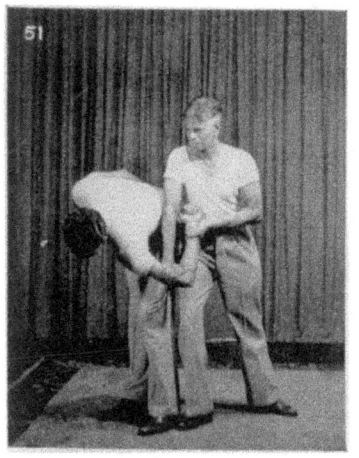
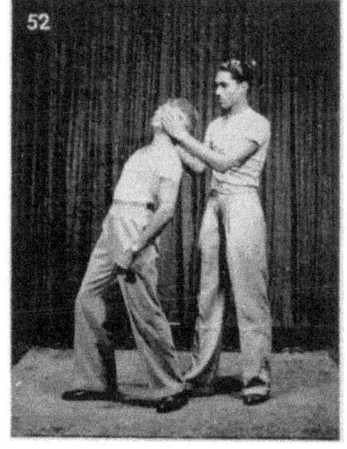

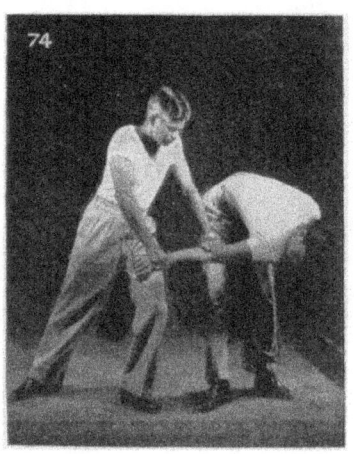

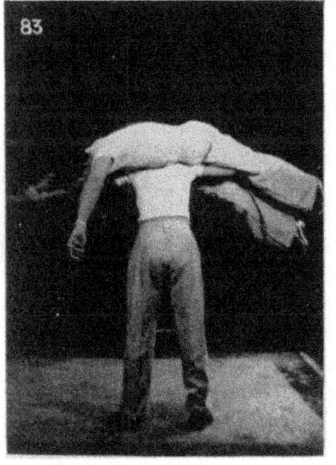

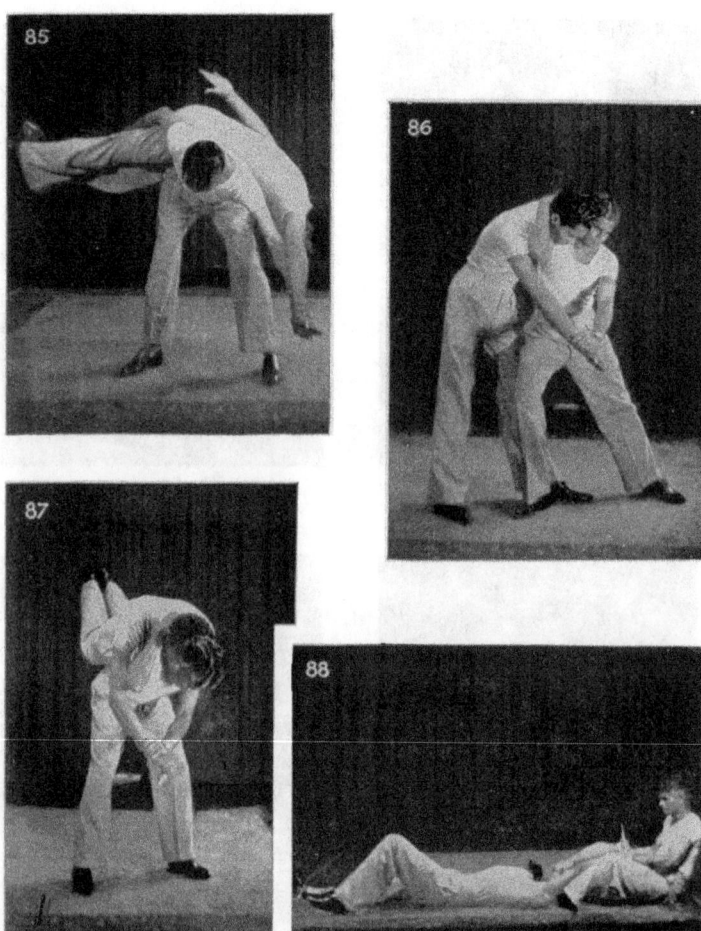

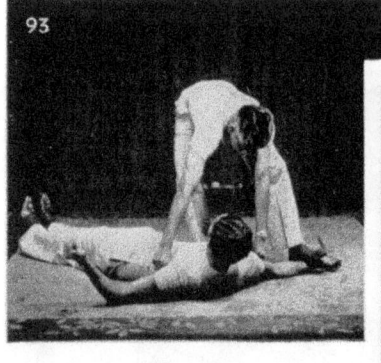

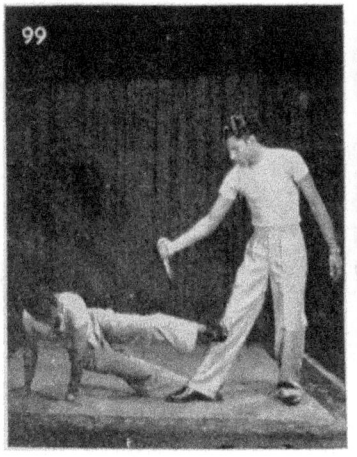

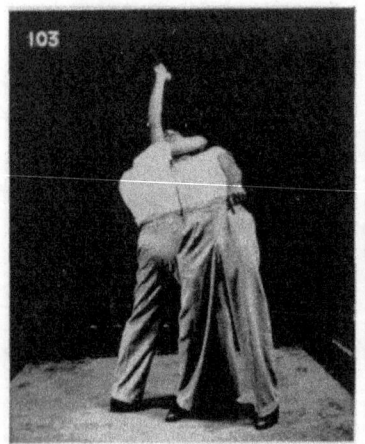

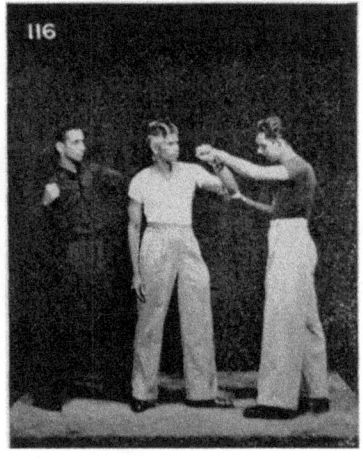

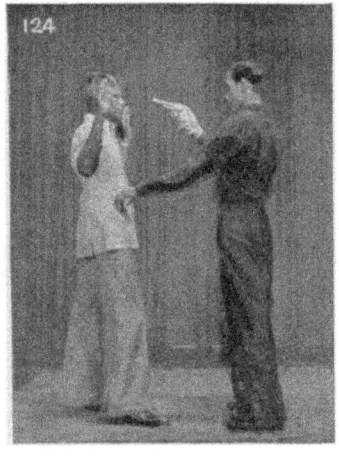

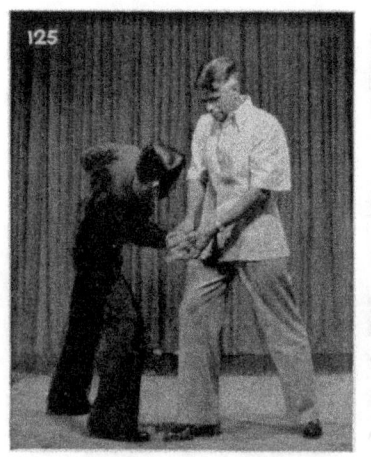

SCIENTIFIC UNARMED COMBAT

lock" on that very arm of his, by a simple process of twisting and turning your arm, to the astonishment of his or your friends who may be witnessing the incident.

When your opponent pulls you as in illustration (50), step forward with your left foot without offering any resistance, hold round his left elbow with your right so that your thumb falls on the nerve-centre of the elbow and the four fingers gripping underneath (*see* No. 13 in chart I, page 85, and No. 3 in chart II). Pinch at the nerve-centre with your right thumb. This will make him suddenly loosen his hold. At the very moment, without relaxing the nerve pinch, twist his arm outwardly towards him by lowering your elbow and raising your forearm with clenched fist at the same time—just as a cobra and polonga (snake) coil in a deadly combat—and turning your palm towards his wrist with outstretched fingers, seize his wrist firmly with your left hand in the same manner as the cobra (after coiling in a deadly combat) would swiftly turn its hood towards the polonga's head to strike. A sudden twist at his captured wrist with your left hand and a simultaneous downward push at his elbow with your right will bring your opponent to position shown in illustration (51).

To lower your elbow and raise your forearm, you should lower your body bending at the knees and waist slightly, taking your chest forward at the same time. When your forearm comes at right angles to the upper arm (in the process of lowering your elbow), turn your palm and apply the "snake-coil-grip".

You will notice that when you lower your elbow and raise the forearm and turn your palm towards his wrist, his arm gets automatically twisted and his grip becomes infirm. Practise this a dozen times or more at a stretch until you have mastered the technique, i.e. when you could apply this grip and hold in a flash without any effort and without causing the least pain to your partner.

If your opponent pulls you with his right hand the same procedure to be adopted reading "right" as "left" and "left" as "right" instead.

Defence 9

SINGLE-HANDED ARM TWIST OR SNAKE-COIL GRIP

When a rowdy or bully seizes your wrist to give you an admonition, in presence of his friends, treating you as a physically inferior person or as a coward, you could apply the same "snake-coil grip" with your captured arm in a jiffy, as explained above. In this instance, when you are not being pulled, you need not use the other hand to hold his elbow. With the application of the "single-handed snake-coil grip", go on twisting his arm until his back is turned towards you. Immediately grip his hair on the back of his head with your free hand and pull him back, whilst at the same time twisting at his wrist. He is now forced to form a semi-circle and strained to look towards the sky; and would yell in pain when his shoulder joint and the whole spinal column begin aching. You may march him forward to any place you want to take him.

Warning

With this snake-coil grip and the hair-grip on, never give the wrist-twist and a sudden jerking pull simultaneously. You may cause a breakage of his spine and damage his shoulder joint as well.

Defence Against Blindfolding from Behind

Defence 10

A Blindfold Shoulder Throw

If an opponent blindfolds you with his hands from behind as in illustration (52), there is a tendency for you to lean back or to be forced to that position. Remember that balance is almighty in self-defence, and the moment you lose your balance you lose the battle. Lower your body therefore immediately, bringing your left foot behind to regain your equilibrium. Seize his left wrist with both your hands, pull him close against your back and bending forward throw him over your left shoulder. If you seize his left wrist you could throw him over your left shoulder [*see* illustration (53)].

CHAPTER FOUR

DEFENCES AGAINST KICKS

There are no safe defences against kicks in wrestling or in boxing. Expert ju-jutsuans who know Kenjutsu and the Japanese Sumo wrestlers, however, have a few defences against kicks.

Legs are the strongest and heaviest limbs of the body and it therefore follows that a kick can be more forceful and deadlier than a blow with the hand on any part of the body except, of course, vital spots.

Whilst fist blows are aimed mostly above the waist, kicks can be delivered on any part of the body ranging from head to foot. Thugs and ruffians are accustomed to kicking. China-footing is the only system that teaches the scientific and systematic art of defence and attack with the legs, and against kicks.

Defence 1

A Leg-Hold Turn-Over Throw

Your opponent attempts to kick you with his right leg as in illustration (54). You immediately side-step to your left and step forward with your right leg, bringing your right hand crossing your body with a circular swinging motion (down and up), so that his outstretched legs come into rest in the crook of your right elbow, as in illustration (55). Raise his entrapped leg with your right arm and he will fall heavily on his back.

You can also catch his right wrist with your left hand, as in illustration (56) and throw him heavily on the ground to his right, by raising his entrapped right leg and pulling his right wrist simultaneously.

Defence 2

ANKLE-HOLD KNEE-BREAKER

As your opponent kicks, turn to your right, revolving on the ball of your left foot, and take your right leg behind. With an upward swinging motion of your left arm from below, divert the kick upwards away from you with your palm in a controlling movement, so that his leg rests in mid-air on your left palm, and thus keep him balancing on one foot. The slightest movement, either by you or by your opponent in this position, will result in his losing his equilibrium and falling back. Immediately his right foot is brought to rest in mid-air, trap his ankle under your right armpit as in illustration (57), and placing your left palm on his knee, apply pressure. This pressure would give him excruciating pain and more pressure would dislocate his knee-joint.

Warning

Never apply sudden pressure on the knee whilst practising.

Defence 3

Standing Leg-Split

After the leg has been trapped under your right armpit, and with downward pressure on his knee, you can switch on to a standing "Leg-Split" by pushing at the side of his left knee with your left foot and pulling his entrapped ankle back with your shoulder as in illustration (58).

Warning

Whilst practising do not raise the right leg high up and do not give too much pressure on the left knee as the hip joint might get dislocated.

CHAPTER FIVE

DEFENCES AGAINST CLUB OR POLE ATTACKS

When a man is infuriated he does not know what he is doing. More often than not, in his desire to revenge himself upon his opponent, he may use anything that he can lay hands on for the purpose of a brutal attack. It may be a chair, a pole, or an iron rod. He will not hesitate to use any of these if he can smash the head of his opponent or attack him otherwise.

Many believe that defence against an iron rod or a pole-attack is well-nigh an impossibility. Faced with a situation of this nature the paramount importance of swift action must again be emphasized.

You will learn some of the finest defences known to this art under this head. All students of the art of self-defence are well advised to master these lessons thoroughly, and also to practise them as often as possible to gain both accuracy and speed.

Defence 1

ARMS-TWIST AND STOMACH-BLOW

Illustration (59) shows your apparently helpless position when you are charged by an opponent who is armed with a rod.

The first idea that should strike your mind is the defensive posture. The right leg is placed forward in this instance. As he delivers you the blow, thrust both your open palms against both elbows of your opponent, so that his elbows alight on the hollow of your palms, and hold the elbows so that your thumbs fall inside and the four fingers overlapping as in illustration (60). Go down a little by bending your knees and elbows to give a spring action to the whole body.

Remember that at any stage your palms should not be brought lower than the level of your head. Pass your right hand quickly over his left wrist and grasp his right wrist from underneath, by turning the palm, so that the little finger edge comes up (palm facing him). Straighten your right arm, and both his arms get twisted as in illustration (61), so that he cannot even drop the rod.

With your free left hand give a knock-out blow at the solar-plexus. It may be a two-finger dig or a left-hand blow with closed fist.

Defence 2

ARMS-TWIST ROD-END DIG

From position in illustration (61), without delivering the knock-out blow, holding the middle of the rod with your left hand, snatch it off from the opponent's locked hands and give a dig with the end of the rod at the solar-plexus.

DEFENCE WITH A WALKING-STICK

Defence 3

A DIG AT TEMPLE

If you happen to be in possession of a walking-stick at the time you are attacked by an opponent, as in the previous defence, the following defences will prove to be very useful :

As the blow is delivered, hold the walking-stick with your hands, well above your head, allowing a space of about 18 inches between your hands, and receive the blow on the middle of your walking-stick as in illustration (62), with similar spring-action as explained in illustration (60). Quickly push his rod forward to his right, and when your stick falls in line with his temple, give a dig with the end of your stick at his temple as in illustration (63). The stick should be slid with your left hand through the grip of your right hand, as the movement of a piston working through a piston-ring.

Defence 4

A Leg-Trip and Push

From position in illustration (63), get closer to your opponent by placing your left leg forward, and maintaining pressure on his rod, give a swinging-back-kick at the back of his right knee with your right leg, as shown in illustration (64) to trip him behind. You can, if you so desire, deliver a blow at your opponent's chest with the end of your stick, as you give the kick to trip him.

Additional Defences

Scrotum-Blow or Knee-Break

As a variation you can, from position in illustration (63), give a kick at your opponent's scrotum or deliver the knee-kick as seen in illustration (97).

Defences Against Club Attacks

Defence 5

An Arm-Lock

Illustration (65) shows that you are on the point of being attacked with a club by your opponent.

An assailant may use, instead of a club, a baton, hatchet or sword. You adjust yourself swiftly to the defensive posture by placing your left leg forward in this instance. Illustration (66) explains how your opponent's hand should be grasped with your left hand as the blow is delivered. Place your right leg forward, and at the same time bring your right hand up from under and give a sharp blow with the wrist bone (little-finger-edge downwards) at the offside of his elbow. This makes his right arm bend inward at the elbow, however strong he may be. You can now either grasp your left wrist or his wrist with your right palm, and raise his bent elbow with your right forearm simultaneously pressing down his wrist with your hand. The effect of the lock would cause severe damage to your opponent's shoulder-blade joints.

Warning

Be extremely careful whilst practising. Avoid the sharp wrist blow and pressure when bending.

Defence 6

A Hand-Twist and Dig-at-Rib

As the blow is being delivered as in illustration (65), you side-step to the left, taking the right leg forward and grasping his wrist in an outward circular motion as it comes down, thus bringing his arm to the position shown in illustration (68). Twist his arm outwardly with your right hand, and with your left raise the club, which will twist your opponent's hand further as in illustration (69), and the club gets released.

Illustration (70) speaks for itself what you should then do. This blow should be aimed at the floating rib.

CHAPTER SIX

DEFENCES AGAINST KNIFE OR DAGGER ATTACKS

Illustration (71) might appear to be rather terrifying at first sight. With the knowledge you have so far gained, and with the self-confidence you have by now acquired, it should not be so to you. Here again the paramount importance of calmness and swift but firm action is emphasized. In contradistinction to the lessons given by some other teachers of this art, the defences described below are not exclusively based on the power of your arms. Legs play an all-important part.

Rhythmical, systematic, side-stepping, dodging, stepping forward, back-stepping, together with the co-ordinated movements of the hands are special features in these defences. Always keep your eyes fixed on your opponent's, except to deceive him by lightning changes in your looks, as occasions demand. You can deceive and puzzle your opponent by fictitious movements of your hands and feet, and by grins as well.

When you gain experience you will be able to read your opponent's next move from his eyes by intelligent anticipation. Always bear in mind that he may change hands, change directions, or may even, whilst threatening you with the knife, resort to other forms of attack, like a blow with the free hand or a kick.

A law-abiding citizen resorts to attack with a knife only when he feels that his chances otherwise are remote. It is no doubt cowardly to use a knife either as a means of attack or defence. When one is being attacked mercilessly and brutally by several unscrupulous ruffians or by robbers, the use of a knife or any other weapon that he can lay hands on, as a last resort, purely for self-protection, cannot be classed as either ungentlemanly or cowardly.

Incidents of this type are not uncommon in all parts of the world.

Defence 1

STRAIGHT-ARM ELBOW-BREAK

In illustration (71) your opponent armed with a dagger (knife) attempts to plunge the deadly weapon into the depths of your heart. You, though fully on the alert, pretend to be very calm. Note carefully illustration (71). As your opponent stabs, you side-step to the left at ninety degrees, the idea being to avert the direction of the knife. Illustration (72) shows how the knife has missed its object. In a split second you grip your opponent's wrist with your right hand, as shown in illustration (73). Bring your left leg forward and, placing your left palm on his right elbow, as in illustration (74), apply pressure.

Warning

Sudden pressure on the elbow of a straightened arm as shown would cause dislocation of the elbow. Do not apply any pressure while practising.

Defence 2

BENT-ARM LOCK

Before your opponent's hand gathers momentum on the downward drive, you, with your legs in the defensive position, grip his wrist with your left hand, as shown in illustration (75). Bring your right leg forward quickly to position shown in illustration (76) and apply the lock at lightning speed, as explained in illustration (67). The front and back views of this lock are clear in illustrations (67) and (76) respectively.

Defence 3

STANDING-LEG LOCK OR KNEE-BREAK

From illustration (75) you can apply the standing-leg-lock, with pressure on the vital spot, just at the joint where the nose meets the upper lip, as in illustration (77). The correct way of applying this "nose-press" is to place the sharp edge of your first finger or thumb at the joint and press in at an angle of 45 degrees. Try this "nose-press" on yourself first.

Defence 4

A Shoulder-Throw

To throw him overhead from position in illustration (73), you can revolve to your right on the ball of your right foot, and taking your opponent's arm over your left shoulder throw him as in illustration (78). The other steps of this throw are explained in illustrations (26) and (27).

Defence 5

A Hip-Throw

Illustration (79) explains another important throw known as the hip-throw. From position in illustration (75) as you bring your right leg forward, move your right hand around his stomach, and placing your hip behind his hip, press him against your body with your palm placed on his back. Stoop your body and lifting your opponent with your hip, throw him whilst simultaneously pulling his wrist, as in illustration (79), so that he falls heavily on his back in front of you. Proceed with the ground-lock, as in illustration (80).

Ground-Lock

As you throw your opponent in front of you remember still to maintain the grip of his captured wrist. Place your left foot on the jugular vein of your opponent's neck, and gripping his captured wrist with both your hands, go down on your right leg. You can then place your right foot against his ribs, and pressing with both your legs, pull the captured arm with both your hands. *See* illustration (80).

Defence 6

Crotch-Hold Roll-over-Shoulders Throw

From position in illustration (75) bring your right leg forward and place same between your opponent's feet. Lowering your body slightly, whilst maintaining a firm grip on his captured wrist, as in illustration (81), shoot your right hand between his legs and under his crotch.

Bring down your opponent's captured wrist over your nape and left shoulder, and holding it firmly with a downward pull, lift him above ground with your right shoulder aided by your right arm, as in illustration (82). You can now roll him over your shoulders, as in illustration (83), so that he falls headlong on the ground with all the fight knocked out of him.

Defence 7

Roll-Over-Back Throw

From position in illustration (75) place your right foot forward and whilst bending down, force his right arm over your back and left shoulder, as in illustration (84). Entwine his right leg from behind with your right arm, and lift him above ground, by raising his right leg and pulling down his right arm simultaneously, whilst straightening your legs, as in illustration (85).

You can now throw him like a dead weight. Give a jerking pull at his captured wrist just at the moment you throw him. Maintain the hold on the captured wrist for further attack if considered necessary.

Defence 8

Nape-Hold Somersault Throw

From position shown in illustration (75) bring your right leg between his legs and lowering his arm with your left-hand grip, bring your right hand around his neck entwining it, and get a firm hold on the nape with your palm, as in illustration (86). Slide your right shoulder under his chest whilst maintaining the firm hold on the nape. Pull him down as you jerk him up with your hip, as in illustration (87), and dash him on the ground somersaulting him right over your shoulder. *See* illustration (88) and proceed with ground-lock.

Ground-Lock

Your opponent in this throw falls so that his legs will be farther away from you, but you will retain your grip on his right wrist with your left hand. Change the grip to your right hand on his right wrist. Immediately grasp his left wrist with your free left hand and place your right foot on his right shoulder. Go down on your left leg to sitting position, and placing the left foot on his left shoulder, pull with your hands whilst pushing with your legs at his shoulders bringing the elbows over your legs.

Warning

More force would seriously damage his shoulders and elbow-joints.

Defence 9

Wrist-and-Cheek Hold Leg-Trip

From the position in illustration (75) bring your right foot just behind his right heel, hooking it as shown in illustration (89). Place your right palm on your opponent's cheek-bone and trip him up to your left whilst pushing him on his cheek with your right and pulling his captured right wrist with your left hand, so that he falls heavily on his back. The purpose of placing your foot behind his heel and hooking it is to prevent him from moving his leg and regaining his balance. The important point is to perform the three steps simultaneously.

Defence 10

Wrist-and-Sleeve Hold Knee-Trip

The three illustrations (91, 92 and 93) explain a similar defence on the same principles as the previous defence. The difference lies in placing the right leg against the side of your opponent's right knee. The hand is not placed on the cheek-bone but grips the right sleeve of your opponent's shirt.

Ground-Lock

As your opponent falls on the ground trample on his right wrist with your left foot and grip his right sleeve with your left fingers in the same manner. You will note that when you have correctly gripped the shirt sleeves you will be in a position to apply pressure on his upper arms either with your knuckles or with the second joints of your fingers. You will also be able to control him in that position and pin him to the ground as in illustration (93).

Your opponent might endeavour to use his left hand to free himself but will be unable to do so as his hands are almost powerless.

Defence 11

Throw-at-Eyes Revolving Knee-Kick

The defence shown in illustrations (94) to (97) is a typical trick in "cheena-adi" self-defence. As your opponent thrusts with his dagger take your right leg behind revolving to your right on the ball of your left foot, as in illustration (94). Stretching your right hand take anything that you can get hold of from the ground, as in illustration (95); be it pebbles, sand or even dust. Keep your eyes fixed on his eyes and still keeping the left hand on guard, as in illustration (95), throw the sand or pebbles or whatever it is in his eyes, as in illustration (96). He will naturally close his eyes; and that is the very moment for you to act. Illustration (97) is self-explanatory. Revolve back forward on the ball of your left foot and deliver the kick at his knee. A kick of this nature may break his leg and put him out of action for a long time to come.

Even if you do not gather any sand or pebbles

or any object to throw in his eyes, that pretended action of throwing and sudden opening of the fingers of your closed fist is sufficient to make him close his eyes. This is a natural instinct of man and beast.

Defence 12

Double-Foot Knee-Breaker

The two illustrations (98) and (99) show another simple but very effective defence.

As your opponent stabs go down on your hands as in illustration (98), hook the back of opponent's right ankle with your right foot. Place your left foot on his knee, as shown in illustration (99) and apply pressure. This will make him fall on the ground. A kick at the knee with the left foot will cause a serious knee-break.

Note :—Going down on your hands should be well timed.

Defence 13

A Knife-Dropping Stomach-Cut

Your opponent in illustration (100) makes use of his left hand either as a defensive or an offensive measure when he attempts to stab you. Make fictitious movements with your hands on the pretext of stopping his left with your right and grasping his right with your left. Bringing your right leg close to his left foot, quickly revolve outward on the ball of your right foot to the left, and deliver a sharp cut with the little-finger-edge of your right hand at his solar-plexus, as in illustration (101). A cut on the solar-plexus will effectively wind him and keep him half bent, grasping his stomach with both his hands, finding it difficult to breathe or straighten his body, as in illustration (102). Never give the "cut" whilst practising with your partner. All the moves should be performed in a flash.

COUNTER: In case you have accidentally given a "cut" to your partner whilst practising, immeiately give the "counter-blow" with the heel of your palm on the centre of his back at the spot just opposite to the solar-plexus. He can then straighten up his body and breathe freely. Then rub down gently at his solar-plexus. If the unfortunate man who receives the "cut" happens to be your assailant, give the "counter-blow" only after administering him a solemn warning, or good advice or whatever it may be.

Defence 14

A JUGULAR-PRESS AND ARM-TRAP

When your opponent stabs at you, side-step to the left, lower your body and thrusting up your right shoulder to come under his armpit, grip him round his neck with your right arm, placing your right leg behind him, hip against hip, as in illustration (103). Apply pressure on the left jugular vein with the narrower side of your wrist bone and lift his right arm with your shoulder. Tightening of the hold would make him giddy in a few seconds. He could be tripped and pushed behind if desired.

Defence 15

Wrist-Pull and Hip-Kick

Illustrations (104) and (105) explain fine cheena-adi feats so easily and quickly performed. This is more spectacular than a flying-mare, from which the armed assailant (being kicked or tripped) goes on toppling for a few seconds and then falling face downwards "bites the dust".

From position in illustration (73) pull your opponent, and just as he goes forward flying past you as in illustration (104), give a sharp (well-timed) side kick at his hip or buttocks, as in illustration (105). Revolve back in a flash on the ball of your left foot and watch how your opponent goes toppling down.

Note:—This is an art in which you have to make use of your opponent's weight, force, movement, apparel, hair, or whatever it is, to your own advantage and to his disadvantage.

For instance, if your opponent rushes at you to stab, when you seize the wrist holding the knife and pull your opponent almost in the same direction, you are making use of his movements and force in this defence to your advantage and to his disadvantage. Study carefully the illustrations (72), (73), (104) and (105).

Defence 16

Wrist-Pull and Trip

This trick is also performed on the same principles. Here, instead of kicking at his hip, you trip him with your right foot at his right ankle just as he goes flying past you after pulling him, as seen in illustration (104).

If you inadvertently fail to bring this trick off, give a sharp kick at his hip or buttocks with your right foot as in illustration (105).

NOTE :—The above is a good example of how you can switch on to another form of attack in a flash if you do not succeed in one. The foot-attacks in cheena-adi self-defence are entirely different from foot-fighting in La Savate.

Defence 17

A Wrist-Parry Knee-kick

Your opponent perhaps attempts to rip open your stomach, as seen in illustration (106). Make fictitious movements with your hands on the pretext of trying to stop his stabbing hand. As the knife descends slant to your right as in illustration (107) to avoid it. Now quickly revolve forward on the ball of your left foot, whilst parrying and pushing his knife-hand with your right, and deliver a kick at his knee (nearest to you), as seen in illustration (108).

NOTE :—When you revolve on the ball of your foot, your whole body should move as a door moves on its hinges.

Defence 18

A Knife-Dropping Nerve-Cut

In illustration (109), as the hand of your opponent comes down, give a sharp cut at the nerve which is about 2 inches from the wrist. This cut will cause your opponent suddenly to stretch his fingers, and the knife will automatically be dropped or thrown off. If this cut is properly delivered it will paralyse his arm for a short while.

Defence 19

Arm-Break Hip-Throw

From position in illustration (75), whilst maintaining your grip of his wrist and placing your right leg behind him, hip behind hip, bring his arm over so that his elbow comes over your nape, and straighten the arm. You can now either break his elbow or throw him to one side or do both, as in illustration (110).

Defence 20

Hand-Twist and Dig

Illustration (111) shows another defence. From position in illustration (75) twist your opponent's hand out lowering it, bring your right leg forward and give a dig with the first two fingers at his solar-plexus. This dig is deadlier than a fist-blow at this spot.

Defence Against Knife Attacks with a Walking-Stick

Although the use of weapons or clubs is not advocated in this art of unarmed combat, yet if you are in possession of a walking-stick it may be

SCIENTIFIC UNARMED COMBAT 77

used with advantage, as shown in the following defence.

Defence 21

Wrist-Parry Elbow-Blow

As your opponent stabs, hold your walking-stick above your head, as shown in illustration (112) (holding the stick a few inches from the two ends).

When his wrist comes in contact with your stick, force his hand down to your left, as shown in illustration (113). Maintaining this pressure with the left hand, give a sharp elbow blow at his temple, as shown in illustration (114). The elbow blow may be given at his jaw bone too.

Defence 22

Hand-Twist and Stick-Dig

From position in illustration (113), maintaining the downward pressure with the stick with your right hand, seize his hand with your left hand, so that the four fingers of your hand overlap the ball of his thumb, and your thumb placed at the back of his palm comes in line between the second and third fingers. Now give a sudden outward twist and dig at the solar-plexus with the end of the walking-stick, as shown in illustration (115).

Defence 23

TWO v. ONE : HAND-TWIST AND ELBOW-DIG

In illustration (116) your assailant comes with an accomplice to attack you. In such a situation you should always bear in mind that there is one, or more, perhaps, behind you to be dealt with. Keep a cool head at all times even if you are faced with an armed gang single-handed. Your hands and legs should then come into action at lightning speed. When you have had constant practice and enough experience, you will marvel how your hands and legs think and act automatically and independently of your brain. A cool head, steel nerves and tricks, in conjunction with a good knowledge of this art, can do wonders in the most difficult situation.

If you are confronted by several opponents, as a rule, give a quick vital-point knock-out blow to the leader first or to the one nearest to you, to send him reeling to the ground. This will certainly have a "stunning" effect on his accomplices and make it easy for you to floor the rest, one by one in quick succession, with your hands and legs.

In illustration (116) your assailant grasps your left hand at the wrist and elbow, with both his hands. His accomplice stands behind you and attempts to catch you round your neck from behind, or to hinder you from taking any offensive action against his friend—your assailant. With a sudden outward twisting turn of your left upper arm (using elbow as a pivot), you could seize your assailant's left wrist which is automatically brought into your left hand as in illustration (117), and go on twisting his arm as seen in the same illustration. At the same time to deliver a knock-out "right elbow-blow" at the other's face or jaw. If the latter happens to be very tall, an elbow-dig can be given at his solar-plexus to silence him. Deal in a suitable way with your assailant who is now at your mercy.

NOTE:—Be extremely careful while practising with your partners not to deliver the dig or to give a sudden twist of the arm.

Defence 24

Two v. One : Neck-Twist and Knee-Kick

In the defences shown in illustrations (118) to (121), a further complication arises when one of the opponents is armed with a knife.

In illustration (118) the assailant aims a knife at you whilst his accomplice attempts to seize you around your neck from behind. You can knock out both in a jiffy with vital point blows without giving them the least chance to cause any injury to you.

Seize the stabbing hand, as seen in illustration

(118), before it gathers momentum, at his wrist with your left hand, and bring it down in the same direction as his arm travels, giving it an inward twist at the same time. Immediately throw your right arm round the accomplice's neck and placing your four fingers on the nearer side of his nose, force his head back with an outward twist to his head so that he may topple over your thigh and leg placed behind him for that purpose. *See* illustration (119). Immediately give a kick at the assailant's knee to disable him. You may not necessarily stick to this order of attacking. Knock-out blows can be given to the accomplice first and then to the assailant or *vice versa* according to circumstances. It does not matter in any way as both the opponents can be knocked out in a matter of two or three seconds or almost simultaneously.

If the nose of the accomplice is out of reach you can catch him by the hair and push his head away from you as in illustration (121). The assailant with knife can of course be severely dealt with by delivering a damaging kick at his knee or an instep kick at his scrotum.

Additional defences :—

Instead of seizing the accomplice's nose or hair, you can give the fatal right elbow-dig at his solar-plexus or a fist-blow at his scrotum with your right hand.

CHAPTER SEVEN

PISTOL DEFENCES

In the illustration (122) your opponent holds you up for some sinister purpose at the point of a revolver. As usual he expects you to surrender by raising both your hands. When doing so remember not to raise your hands above the level of your head. By all means show him that you have surrendered and are prepared to obey any of his commands. Never lose courage. It should be your scheme to capture though you pretend to be captured.

Do not give your opponent the faintest inkling that you have in mind to overpower him, lest he should be still more careful not to give you the slightest chance. One wrong move would cost you your life.

When your opponent is confident that you are not the type who would try to offer resistance or be aggressive, he will, with his free hand, search your pockets. Allow him to do so, and while he is at it is the time for you to act swiftly and effectively.

82 SCIENTIFIC UNARMED COMBAT

Defence 1

WRIST-GRIP AND THROAT-AXE

In a flash seize your opponent's right wrist with your left hand and, bringing your left leg forward at the same time, push his hand down so that the barrel of the revolver points away from you.

Now bring your right leg forward and give a sharp cut at his Adam's apple, as in illustration (123). This cut is known as the "Throat-axe".

Warning :—Never administer the "Throat-axe" while practising.

Defence 2

BENT-ARM WRIST-BREAKER

In illustration (124) your opponent, presumably in haste and with the utmost confidence in his revolver, aims at your head almost point blank. He utilizes his other hand to remove your belongings from your pocket. He tries to take whatever he can and get away quickly.

Seize his right wrist in a flash with your right hand (slanting to your right at the same time) and giving it an outward twist. Immediately grasp his right hand with your left (the four fingers overlapping his thumb and your thumb placed on the outside of his palm, as explained in illustration

(115); give a further twist to his hand to bend it at his wrist. Now slide your right hand up bringing your right thumb side-by-side with your left thumb, and go on twisting with both your hands as in illustration (125). Further pressure or a sudden twist will cause a dislocation of his wrist.

Defence 3

Wrist-Hold, Trip-and-Push

Illustration (126) explains an additional defence. Seize his right wrist with your left hand from position shown in illustration (124), and take your right leg behind his right leg to prevent him from moving. With the hollow of your palm placed under his chin give a push immediately. Changing the grip at his wrist with your right palm as he falls, twist his hand with both your hands, as explained in the previous defence. His grip of the revolver will get loosened by your twist and the revolver will drop to the ground.

Defence 4

Double-Arm-Twist Arm-Lock

Illustration (127) explains a further defence. From position in illustration (124), swiftly grip the pistol entrapping his finger in the trigger guard and give a sudden push upwards.

Bring your right forearm above his left forearm and pass same alongside his body under his left upper-arm. Now with a slight outward twist of your arm and placing the wrist at the back of his upper arm, hook it with your fist. With an upward jerk on his forearm with your forearm, and a little downward pressure with your hooked fist on his upper arm, you could bend his arm at the elbow as in illustration (127). At the same time, with ease you could bring his right arm bent over his neck, as in the same illustration. This will cause severe pain to every inch of his body above his waist.

All photographs from Nos. 4 to 128 reproduced in this book are by TURRET STUDIOS, Ltd., Kollupitiya, COLOMBO, CEYLON.

SCIENTIFIC UNARMED COMBAT

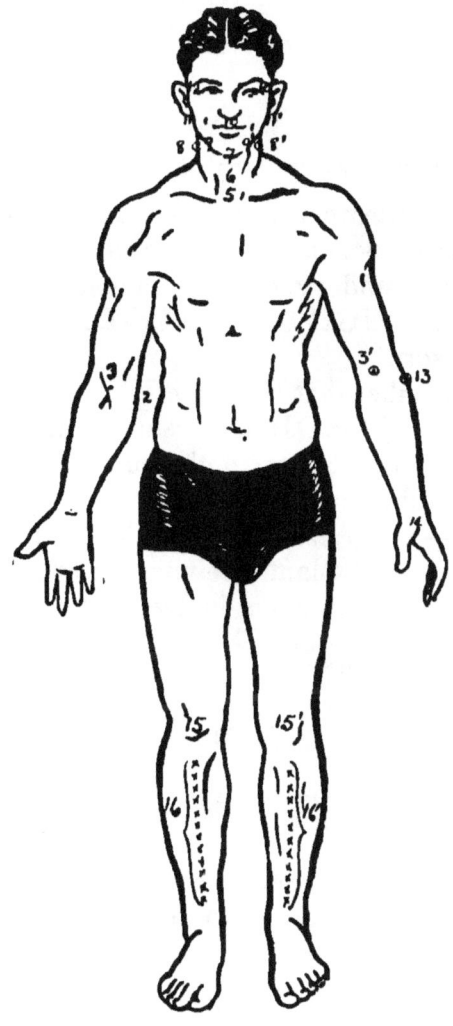

Chart 1

CHART 1

Given in the order of their vulnerability

A

Nos. 4—5—6—10—12—12^1.

Never attempt to attack your assailant or assailants on the spots mentioned above, unless you are compelled, under very trying circumstances, to exercise your RIGHT OF SELF-DEFENCE, as a last resort.

Remember that these are VITAL TOUCHES (VARMA-ADI), the results of which would invariably prove fatal if the cuts, blows or digs alight on the exact spots.

NOTE :—Study carefully the COUNTER blow to revive an assailant receiving a blow, cut or dig on No. 4, as explained in Defence 13, page 72, chapter VI, under *"Defences against knife or dagger attacks"*.

B

Nos. 7—8—8^1—9—9^1—11—11^1—15—15^1—16—16^1.

Resort to these only when you are attacked by dangerous criminals, or to extricate yourself from a tight corner when being attacked by a number of men, or in exercising the RIGHT OF SELF-DEFENCE.

A cut, blow, dig or kick (as the case may be) correctly delivered on the identical spots will knock out any assailant instantly.

C

Nos. 1—2—3—7—10—11—11^1—12—12^1—13—14—15—15^1—16—16^1.

Nerve pinches, nerve presses, cuts, blows or digs when correctly applied or administered on these spots (as the case may be) will have a deadly effect on any opponent. Anyone can be made to remain motionless or be put out of action temporarily. A kick with the tip or heel of the shoe on 15—15^1, or on any spot in the bracket 16—16^1, will bring about the same result.

Warning

Never give a hard blow on points 10—12—12^1 and 7—11—11^1 as stated under A and B respectively. Just a mild pressure with the thumb or first finger on 10, or pressure with the second joints of your first and second fingers on 7—12—12^1, or a thrust with the index finger (held rigidly) at 11 or 11^1 (which is the depression at the end of the jaw-bone behind the ear-lobe), will be quite sufficient to obtain the desired effect.

88 SCIENTIFIC UNARMED COMBAT

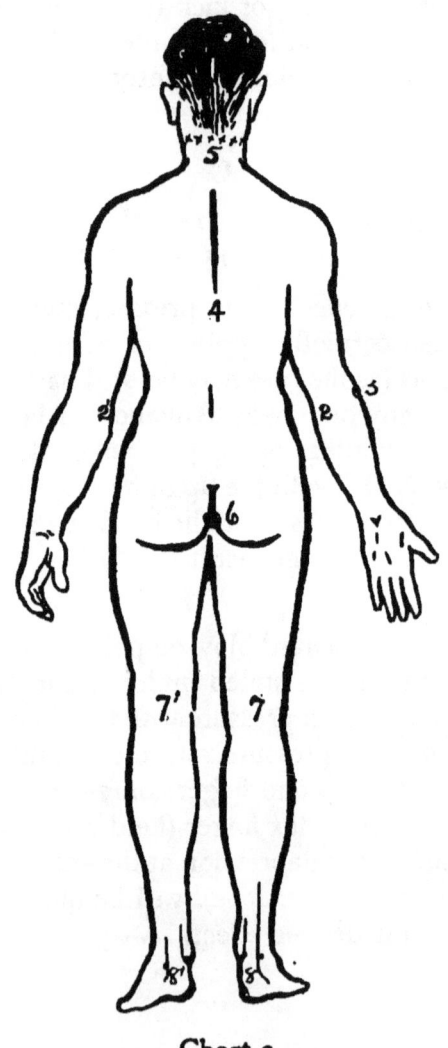

Chart 2

CHART 2

Given in the order of their vulnerability

D

No. 6.

It is well advised to avoid causing any injury to one's coccyx. A kick or a backward fall on hard ground or object could cause severe injury to that part of the anatomy. Bear in mind that a damaged coccyx cannot be cured unless removed by surgical treatment.

No. 5.

A cut with the little-finger-edge of the hand at the base of the skull is much more deadly than a fist blow at that spot, and will send even the strongest man reeling to the ground.

Nos. 2—2^1.

These are the ends of the two funny bones at the elbows. A hard knock at them with the second joint of the second finger of the closed fist will totally disable the opponent's arm for several minutes.

Never try any of these as a means of attack on any person other than a hardened criminal.

E

Nos. 1—8—8^1—3—7—7^1.

These are points where nerve pinches can be applied with deadly effect. Any strong, boisterous or dangerous criminal can be silenced or brought under absolute control with a vice-like grip, with your first finger and thumb held around 1 or 8.

You can pinch or press with your thumb on 3—7—7^1 while the four fingers are placed around in support.

F.

No. 4.

This is the spot where a "counter" blow has to be given immediately after a "cut" or "dig" on (4) in chart 1, in order to revive the victim.

CONCLUSION

I have laid bare a good number of secrets and their detailed manipulation in this UNARMED COMBAT which other teachers have not explicitly touched upon. A keen student of this noble art of self-defence, who has earnestly practised these defences, studied and mastered my technique should know HOW, WHEN, WHERE and on WHOM to administer these nerve-pinches and vital point blows. The student should also have by now acquired complete SELF-RELIANCE and SELF-CONTROL. Even at this stage I feel it is not inappropriate to remind one to be extremely cautious in the exercise of these vital-point blows, as their indiscreet use would defeat the very noble purpose they are intended to serve. Finally I should ask every student scrupulously to observe the ten precepts at all times. The more knowledge and experience one acquires in this scientific art the more cool-headed and self-reliant he should become.

THE END

A Selection Of Classic Instructive Titles Relating
To The Art Of Pugilism & Self Defence
In Both War & Peace
Find our entire selection @ naval-military-press.com

ALL-IN FIGHTING
The distilled knowledge of W.E. Fairbairn, legendary SOE instructor in unarmed combat, and inventor of the Sykes-Fairbairn knife, who learned his deadly skills in 30 years on the Shanghai waterfront. Fully illustrated.
9781847348531

ART OF BOXING AND SCIENCE OF SELF DEFENCE
Former Lightweight Champion Billy Edwards shares the techniques and strategies of the sweet science in his beautifully illustrated boxing guide. Explore boxing's transition from bare knuckle spectacle to today's Marquis of Queensbury ruleset.
9781474539548

SELF DEFENCE OR THE ART OF BOXING

Ned Donnelly was a pioneer of boxing training during the late Victorian era. Explore the strategies and techniques used by this trainer of champions via a series of easy-to-follow illustrations and clear, concise coaching steps.

9781474539562

JACK GOODWIN'S BOXING

This 1920's boxing masterpiece by Jack Goodwin puts you in the shoes of a coach in that era. Uncover the best ways to run, manage and train boxers as taught by Jack Goodwin, a champion and trainer of champions in the noble science.

9781474539586

THE COMPLETE BOXER

Gunner Moir provides detailed instructions on the techniques he deployed to become British Heavyweight Champion. Taught in a series of easy to learn techniques, combinations, and boxing strategies.

9781474539609

ART OF WRESTLING
George de Relwyskow Army Gymnastic Staff

In the appreciation to this book Captain Daniels, V.C., M.C., Rifle Brigade, states: "In adding a word to this book on the style of wrestling as taught at the Headquarters Gymnasium of the British Army, and having had personal experience in the various holds and throws taught, I consider it has been of great value in the training of the soldier, and the bringing out of those qualities of grit and determination which have been seen in all ranks who have taken an active part throughout the greatest war in history." 1919.

9781783313563

KILL OR GET KILLED

Rex Applegate's "kill or be killed" helped prepare America's marines, soldiers, sailors, spies and airmen for the realities of war. This highly shared and respected work provides all you need to know about unarmed combat and close quarter engagement with the enemy.

9781474539661

BOXING (V-Five)
The Aviation Training Office of the Chief of Naval Operations
The game-changing V-Five suite of training manuals helped get a generation of American aviators fit for war. Here we explore how the airmen of the US navy trained in boxing as part of their military fitness regime.
9781474539623

THE TEXTBOOK OF WRESTLING
Get your wrestling skills matt-ready from wrestling champion and world-renown trainer Ernest Gruhn. Replete with detailed holds, throws, pins and strategies for success in a wide range of wrestling rulesets.
9781474539647

MANUAL OF PHYSICAL TRAINING 1914
(United States Army)
Published just prior to the outbreak of World War 1, this beautifully illustrated guide was designed to revolutionise the combat fitness and readiness of the US Army covering a wide range of gymnastic and combat calisthenic exercises.
9781474539708

DEAL THE FIRST DEADLY BLOW
United States Department of the Army
This Vietnam-era classic showcases in detail how the US Forces trained in close quarter combat. Known as the "encyclopaedia of combat" it helped a generation learn how to become devastating effective with empty hands, knives and bayonets alike.
9781474539722

HAND-TO-HAND COMBAT
Bureau of Aeronautics U.S Navy 1943

This is one of the best combative manuals from World War 2, developed by the US Navy V-Five Staff, that included the renowned American wrestler Wesley Brown. It is then not especially surprising that wrestling skills predominate in this manual, and form the base skill-set for this combative system.

9781474537391

ABWEHR ENGLISCHER GANGSTER METHODEN DEFENSE OF ENGLISH GANGSTERS METHODS – SILENT KILLING – FULL ENGLISH TRANSLATION

In 1942 the Wehrmacht published a training manual with the goal of countering the "silent killing" tactics used by the British commando units. The manual was – much in line with typical National Socialist terminology –titled

"Abwehr Englischer Gangster-methoden" or "Defence Against English Gangster methods".

This book was compiled due the Wehrmacht intelligence operatives uncovering of a British hand-to-hand course for the SOE, Commandos, et al, on methods of quick and silent killing (undoubtedly developed by W. E. Fairbairn and E. A. Sykes). They correctly assessed that their troops in general and particularly the Geheime Staatspolizei (Gestapo), Sicherheitsdienst (SD), their security guards, and sentries would be in grave danger when confronted by men trained in these methods. This manual/program was the Wehrmacht's response.

9781474538336

BOXING FOR BOYS
Regtl. Sergt.-Major & B Dent Army Gymnastic Headquarters

A successful system of boxing instruction for large classes, to allow tuition with no detriment to the "backward or shy pupil". Covers Kit-On, Guard-Sparring-Advance-Point & Mark-Ducking-Medicine, Bag-Left & Right Hooks etc. The author considered that boxing systematically taught to the youth was beneficial exercise, and would have a marked elevating influence on the national character.

9781783314607

HAND-TO-HAND FIGHTING
A System Of Personal Defence For The Soldier (1918)

A tough book on the art of hand to hand fighting in the trenches of the Great War. Demonstrating techniques utilised to "do away with the enemy", many of which are barred in clean wrestling, the book includes good clear photographic illustrations presenting important attack methods including the "Hammer Lock", "Kidney Kick", "Head Twist", "Knee Groin Kick", and the "Knee Break", all very important in a man to man, life or death encounter, when fighting in the mud of the trenches.

9781783313983

HAND TO HAND COMBAT

Francois d'Eliscu taught thousands of U.S. Army Rangers how to fight down and dirty in World War II. d'Eliscu doesn't get the press that Fairbairn and Applegate do, but he did a commendable job writing this book. It is basic, meant for training raw recruits in a short amount of time before sending them to the front, but simple is good when you are in combat, as most combative experts' will tell you.

9781474535823

COLD STEEL

A cold-war combatives classic. John Styers, US Marine and WW2 veteran, lays out his approach to close quarters combat with rifle, bayonet, stick, knife and empty hands. Explore what helped wartime and post-war Marines stay ahead of the competition with lucid imagery and clear combative descriptions.

9781474540643

THE COMPLETE KANO JIU-JITSU

Join world-famous physical culture expert H. Irving Hancock, and Jiu-Jitsu specialist Katsukama Higashi as they showcase the art of 'Kano Jiu-Jitsu' now known as Judo. Get an exclusive glimpse into the transitional era of the martial art, alongside how it uses Japanese physical culture methodologies for self-improvement.

9781474540735

WE Fairbairn's Complete Compendium of Lethal, Unarmed, Hand-to-Hand Combat Methods and Fighting In Colour

All 844 images of Fairbairn and his assistants can now for the first time be seen in full colour, lending a clarity to the practical methods of mastering the manner of dealing with an assailant, both in time of war and when placed in difficulty during unpleasant modern urban situations. These various holds, trips, kicks, blows etc, allow the average man or woman a position of security against almost any form of armed or unarmed attack. Captain W.E. Fairbairn would have approved of this new colour version, that gives an illustrative clarity to the original that was lacking in previous monochrome reprints of his work.

All six of W.E. Fairbairn's works in one binding to create the ultimate colour compendium: Get Tough-All-In Fighting-Shooting to Live-Scientific Self-Defence-Hands Off!-Defend

9781783318735

SELF DEFENCE FOR WOMEN COMBATO

Join the Canadian combatives legend William "Bill" Underwood as he showcases self-defence for women. Over the course of clear photography, sketches and instructions he lays out a curriculum for self-defence for the attacks women would be most likely to face.

9781474540711

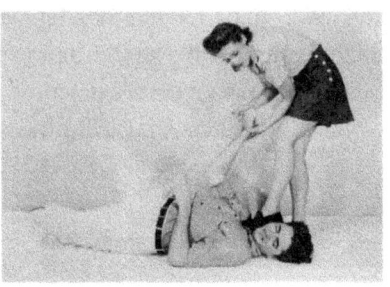

SCIENTIFIC UNARMED COMBAT
The Art of Dynamic Self-Defence

Learn the esoteric Sri Lankan art of 'Cheena-Adi' with R. A Vairamuttu. This guide explores armed and unarmed self-defence drawing heavily from Indian martial culture, alongside wellness and development from Indian physical culture, fitness, diet and medicine.

9781474540728

THE NEW SCIENCE
Weaponless Defence

Join wrestling champions Prof F. S Lewis, William V Gregory and Boxing Champ Tommy Burns as they showcase street orientated self-defence from people with a proven track record of fighting success. This 1906 manual via a series of photos and instructions lays out simple, tried and tested ways to keep yourself safe.

9781474540704

COMBAT CONDITIONING MANUAL
Jiu-Jitsu Defence, Bayonet Defence and Club Defence

This 1942 guide for marines lays out the basics of combat Ju Jitsu as part of an overall training regimen for US Marines. It's a holistic guide that covers defences against armed and unarmed attackers, physical fitness and even first aid.

9781474540698

BOXING TAUGHT THROUGH "SLOW MOTION FILM"

Learn the ropes from the best fighters of the 1900s-1930s in this unique boxing manual. Using stills from super slow-mo fight footage, this treasure trove unpacks the skills, tips and tactics of the champs for you to emulate at home.

9781474540681

HOW TO BOX CORRECTLY

Explore the art of boxing according to famous Bronx boxing brand Ben Lee in this 1944 how-to guide. Learn the ropes from one of the nation's top trainers and boxing journalists John J. Romano, in this warmly illustrated guide to the sweet science.

9781474540674

www.ingramcontent.com/pod-product-compliance
Lightning Source LLC
Chambersburg PA
CBHW070456090426
42735CB00012B/2576